Author:

Fiona Macdonald studied history at Cambridge University and at the University of East Anglia. She has taught children, adults and undergraduates. She has written many books on historical topics, mainly for children.

Illustrators:

David Antram was born in Brighton in 1958. He studied at Eastbourne College of Art and then worked in advertising for 15 years before becoming a full-time artist. He has illustrated many children's non-fiction books.

John James was born in London in 1959. He studied at Eastbourne Collage of Art and specialised in historical reconstruction since leaving art school in 1982.

Series creator:

David Salariya is an illustrator, designer and author. He is the founder of the Salariya Book Company, which specialises in the creation and publication of books for young people, from babies to teenagers, under its imprints Book House, Scribblers and Scribo.

Editor: **Jenny Millington**

Published by
Book House, an imprint of
The Salariya Book Company Ltd
25 Marlborough Place, Brighton BN1 1UB

SALARIYA

Visit
www.salariya.com
for our online catalogue and
free fun stuff.

ISBN 978-1-908973-62-7

A CIP catalogue record for this book is available from the British Library.

Printed and bound in China.
Printed on paper from sustainable forests.
Reprinted in MMXVIII.

CONTENTS

A Samurai Castle

Written by
Fiona Macdonald

Series created by
David Salariya

Illustrators
David Antram
John James

BOOK HOUSE
a SALARIYA imprint

INTRODUCTION

IF YOU WERE a time-traveller, visiting Japan at any moment during the past 400 years, you could hardly fail to be impressed by its magnificent castles. These castles were mostly built during the 16th and 17th centuries, for samurai (warrior) families. During that time, many castles were erected, and thousands of skilled workers were employed to construct them. Why were these castles built? How were they made without modern cranes, bulldozers and earth-moving machinery? Who paid for them, and where did the money come from? What was it like to live, work, fight and sometimes die within their walls? You can find the answers to these questions – and many others – in this book.

Only a few samurai castles survive today. Their carefully preserved remains can tell us a great deal about building methods and construction details. But we can find out more – about the thoughts, feelings and behaviour of the people who built them – from contemporary documents giving detailed descriptions of samurai warriors and their lifestyle, and from Japanese pictures painted on scrolls and beautiful folding screens.

WHO WERE THE SAMURAI?

SAMURAI were warriors and landowners, who lived in Japan. From the 12th to the 18th centuries, they were the most powerful group of people in the country.

Samurai were rich, because they had land. It was farmed by peasants who grew rice to give to the samurai as rent. Rice was the chief form of wealth in Japan. Samurai had weapons – the samurai badge of rank was a daisho, or matching pair of swords. Even samurai women wore a dagger tucked into the wide silk sashes around their waists.

Above all, samurai had private armies, which gave them the power to do what they liked – as long as rival samurai did not try to stop them. Samurai admired, feared and respected one another, but the only man they obeyed was the shogun, the national army commander-in-chief.

However, samurai were more than just fighters. They were members of a ruling class who prided themselves on their ancestry, bravery and sense of honour, as well as on their fighting skills. Samurai were born, not made. To be a real samurai, you had to have samurai parents; occasionally, a man might be adopted into a samurai family, but only if he had shown himself worthy of such a noble reward.

In 1592, samurai warriors led 200,000 Japanese soldiers to invade Korea. They were successful at first, but were soon forced to retreat when the mighty Chinese empire came to Korea's aid.

The samurai Minamoto Yoritomo (1147–1198) was a great warlord. By 1185, after five years of fighting, Yoritomo won control of most of Japan. Recognising his power, the Japanese emperor made him 'Sei-i Tai Shogun' (Great General Subduing the Barbarians).

Officially, Yoritomo was leader of all the emperor's warriors, with a special duty to defend Japan from invaders. But, in fact, he was more powerful even than that. For the next 700 years, shoguns, not emperors, were the real rulers of Japan.

AMERICA
JAPAN
CHINA
RUSSIA
EUROPE
AFRICA

The land of Japan is made up of hundreds of islands. This map (right) shows the four largest, where most people live. The land on these islands is rocky and mountainous; it could be difficult to travel from one region to another, especially in winter, when snow blocked the mountain paths. This rugged landscape made Japan hard to govern; each remote area had its own warlord. In theory, they were loyal to the emperor and the shogun – but they valued their independence as well.

SEA OF JAPAN

HOKKAIDO

Hirosaki castle

HONSHU

PACIFIC OCEAN

Bitchu-Matsuyama castle

Osaka

Kyoto

SHIKOKU

KYUSHU

• Edo (now Tokyo)

Kochi castle

Matsuyama castle

In 1600, Tokugawa Ieyasu feared that rival samurai were plotting to overthrow him. To make sure he stayed in control, he seized the castles belonging to 87 samurai families, and banished many others to outlying lands (shown in orange).

JAPANESE SOCIETY

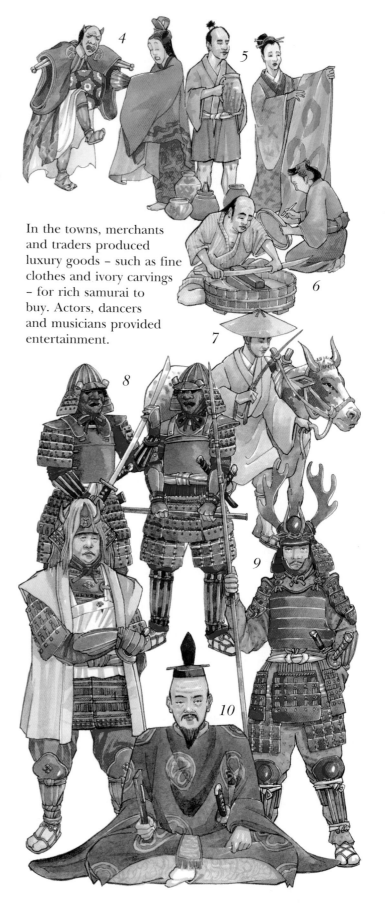

ALTHOUGH SAMURAI were the most powerful group in Japan, they were not the most high-ranking. The emperor was at the top of society, refined, remote and godlike, and believed to be descended from the sun. The shogun, who ruled for the emperor, came next in rank. Originally, shoguns had been chosen for their skill as war leaders. But after 1603, all shoguns came from one ruling dynasty, founded by the shogun Tokugawa Ieyasu, who lived from 1542 to 1616. By defeating any samurai who dared oppose him, he brought peace to Japan after years of civil war. Samurai had the next highest status, but they were not all equal.

In the towns, merchants and traders produced luxury goods – such as fine clothes and ivory carvings – for rich samurai to buy. Actors, dancers and musicians provided entertainment.

Japanese society:
(1) Buddhist priest
(2) Buddhist monk
(3) Buddhist nun
(4) Actors
(5) Town traders
(6) Country craftsmen
(7) Farmer
(8) Low-ranking soldiers (ashigaru) in a samurai's private army
(9) High-ranking samurai (daimyo)
(10) The shogun, leading warlord and ruler of all Japan.

The emperor's court:
(A) Useful people: maids, servants, cooks, cleaners
(B) Scribes, clerks and officials
(C) Old noble families, some holding ancient honorary posts
(D) The emperor.

From AD 794, the emperor and his court lived in the ancient capital city of Kyoto. There they led an elegant life, following ancient traditions, but had no political power. That was based at the shogun's castle, and, after 1603, at the shogun's new capital city of Edo (present-day Tokyo).

Top samurai, called 'daimyo' (lords), owned great estates and fine castles. There were also lower-class samurai, who fought as officers in daimyo private armies. Next in rank came ordinary soldiers, or 'ashigaru'.

The peasants who farmed the daimyo's estates were often very poor. But they ranked next after the samurai and ashigaru, because they produced rice to feed everyone else in Japan. Buddhist priests, monks and nuns might be respected, but only if they came from families of samurai rank. Craftworkers and merchants were at the bottom of the social scale.

1 — 1576

2 — 1579

3 — 1601/1620

4 — 1606

Choosing the Site

THE EARLIEST castle builders chose sites that were easy to defend – mountain crags or rocky cliffs. The first forts and castles were simply strong walls around a central keep (or 'tenshu') for warlords and their soldiers to take refuge.

When Yoritomo became shogun in 1185, he needed help to rule the country. He recruited loyal samurai, made them daimyo, and gave them land. These top-rank samurai built splendid, more spacious castles throughout Japan to house their family in comfort, and to accommodate their soldiers, servants and officials. New castle sites were chosen, too. Some were still in the mountains, others were in lowland valleys or on coastal plains. There, castles could guard the roads and rivers connecting daimyo territories with hostile neighbouring lands, where enemy samurai patrolled. Many new sites lacked strong natural defences, but artificial barriers could quickly be built.

Most samurai castles have disappeared. Shown above are eight of the surviving ones with the dates when they were built:
(1) Maruoka
(2) Matsumoto
(3) Inuyama
(4) Hikone
(5) Himeji
(6) Matsue
(7) Marugame
(8) Uwajima.

Before the tenshu or strong central keep could be built, its outer defences had to be planned by professional architects. In mountainous areas, or on steep river banks, loose rocks and slippery slopes formed natural barriers against attack.

On lowland castle sites, high, steep banks of earth were heaped up, deep moats were dug, and strong outer walls were constructed. Foundations were laid, on which gatehouses and tall watchtowers could be built.

Outer wall

Moat

Bridge over moat

Stone walls

Bird's-eye view of Himeji ('White Egret') castle

5   1609

6   1611

7   1660

8   1665

The simplest castles were built with a single tenshu (keep) – see castles 1, 7 and 8 above.

The most elaborate castles had two or more smaller tenshu joined on to the central one – see castles 2 and 5.

Larger, more complicated castles were built with several small towers next to the tenshu – see castles 3, 4 and 6.

Watchtower

Tenshu (keep)

Gatehouse

Inner stone walls

BUILDING THE CASTLE

'Disordered piling' was made of small stones packed tightly together, leaving no cracks for attackers to find footholds.

'Burdock piling' was made of large, carefully shaped blocks fitted together over a mound of earth. Cracks were filled with pebbles.

Castle walls were built without mortar, so each stone could move slightly without the whole building cracking.

Many walls were built with a curved profile, rather than a straight edge. This also increased their stability during an earthquake.

SAMURAI CASTLES were built by hand. The huge boulders used to construct walls had to be rough-hewn at quarries or collected from mountainsides, then sorted, lifted and fitted together without the help of power-driven machinery. They also had to be carried to castle building sites. Often, paths were too steep to use wheeled carts, so everything had to be carried in baskets slung from poles.

Enormous quantities of stone were used: the walls encircling Himeji Castle (1609) have a surface area of over 100,000 square metres (1 million square feet). These walls were usually left rough but a few castles have stonework with a very smooth finish. Inside the walls, castle buildings were made of wood and plaster. The strong timber framework was prefabricated at a master carpenter's workshop, then assembled at the castle site. The standard of woodwork was very high, with precision joints and intricately carved doors, window frames and rafters. Stonemasons and carpenters were very well trained, and were proud of their traditional skills. Boys were apprenticed to a master craftsman at 13, and spent many years learning their craft.

Carpenters used saws and chisels like these to cut and shape the timbers used to build castles' interior walls.

Castle building was supervised by a bugyo, or overseer. He was trained in traditional skills. It was his duty to respect and preserve them, and to pass them on to future generations.

Instructions for making a roof, 1658 (above).

Walls were covered with wood strips, hemp and plaster (below).

Builders took special care with corner stones of walls. They were wedged together in an interlocking pattern for extra strength.

Walls with zigzag corners were extra-strong, and also very decorative. Japanese builders called them 'folding fans'.

Top samurai had their castle walls built curving upwards. This was a sign of wealth and status. It was also thought to look good.

13

CASTLE DESIGN

THE PERIOD 1570–1690 is often called the 'Golden Age' of Japanese castle building. Unlike traditional Japanese buildings, they were several storeys high. For example, the keep in Matsumoto castle (completed 1596) had floors on six levels. 'Golden Age' castles were also admired for their innovative layout. They were planned as clusters of towers, and included features like gateways, courtyards, reception halls, borrowed from all kinds of traditional buildings, from temples to townhouses.

The resulting castles were very beautiful, with carved and painted woodwork and steep, soaring roofs. The outer walls of Matsue castle (completed 1611) were covered in shiny black lacquer, earning it the nickname 'Raven Castle'. Hikone castle (completed 1603) was decorated in gold. Himeji castle (completed 1609) was covered in special, fireproof white plaster. This, plus its graceful, curving gables, won it the name 'White Egret Castle'. Until the early 17th century, these magnificent castles had an extra purpose: to display samurai power. That is why, in 1615, shogun Ieyasu banned samurai from building more than one castle on each of their estates.

100 metres
(328 feet)

(1) Moat
(2) Outer walls
(3) Outer bailey
(4) Inner walls
(5) Kitchens, stables, workshops, rest rooms for soldiers
(6) Inner bailey
(7) Watchtower
(8) Side tower
(9) Minor gatehouse
(10) Fortified passage
(11) Keep containing: main hall for receiving visitors; offices for daimyo's administrative staff; watchtower and gun storage room; kitchens and food stores; daimyo's living rooms; soldiers' rooms
(12) Impressive roof
(13) Fine plastered walls.

Shown here is Himeji castle, built in 1609. The small picture opposite shows a plan of the castle and its surroundings.

12

13

11

10

8

9

7

6

15

ELEGANT INTERIORS

TRADITIONALLY, Japanese houses did not have solid dividing walls. The inner space was partitioned by wood and paper screens, which could be moved as required to create areas for living, sleeping or eating.

The space inside a castle was arranged in much the same way. Originally, strength and security were the prime consideration for samurai but soon, castle interiors began to be planned – at least in part – as showcases for their owner's wealth, good breeding and excellent taste.

Laws passed by the shogun stated that only samurai families could buy luxury goods. A beautiful, well-furnished castle became visible proof of high rank. Screens, decorated with paintings of plants, birds and flowers in glowing colours and glittering with gold, separated important visitors from the 'working' parts of the keep. Rafters overhead were carved and painted, and furnishings – tables, chests, dishes and serving bowls – were exquisitely made from rare woods, lacquerware and fine porcelain. Like the outside of a castle, the inside was designed to impress.

2

One of the finest screen paintings of the samurai period is at Nijo castle.

It shows pine trees set against a shimmering golden background.

The ceiling is decorated with birds perched on red and white flowers.

Wells supplied essential drinking water. They were kept carefully guarded. Himeji had ten wells.

Diagonal braces, cut from thick beams of wood, strengthened the corner posts of tall castles.

Inner walls were lightweight, movable screens. Outer walls had holes for shooting at enemies.

Well-defended doors: this door from Himeji Castle had locks, bolts, and iron armour-plating outside.

Rich homes would prize beautiful, useful objects like these soup bowls and sweet dishes, or this sake (rice-wine) bottle, shaped like an aubergine. All are made of lacquer.

Mats, called tatami, covered castle floors, and were used for sitting or sleeping. They were made of rice-husks sandwiched between two layers of tightly woven reeds.

The richer you were, the thicker the mats you could afford. Mats in the emperor's palace were almost 50 per cent thicker than in ordinary homes.

Because everyone sat or knelt on the floor, tables and chests were built low.

PEOPLE OF THE CASTLE

ONE HISTORIAN has calculated that castle-building was the biggest industry in 16th- and 17th-century Japan. Constructing, decorating, repairing and maintaining castles employed a great many people, from the bugyo (high-ranking commissioner of works) to the lowliest labourers.

A large number of people were also needed to keep a castle running from day to day. As well as being a fortress, a castle was a home, so servants were employed to cook, clean, mend clothes, care for children, and wait on the samurai family. There might also be poets and musicians to entertain them.

(1) Peasant farmer
(2) Weaver
(3) Basketmaker
(4) Blacksmith
(5) Leatherworker
(6) Porter
(7) Potter
(8) Swordsmith

(9) Estate manager
(10) Builder
(11) Architect
(12) Screen-painter
(13) Widowed grandmother
(14) Samurai's wife
(15) Maid
(16) Son and heir
(17) Daughter

The women of a samurai family lived in private quarters, far removed from the workmen and peasants coming from the rough world outside, and from the soldiers guarding the castle. The higher the samurai's rank, the more important it was to shelter 'his' women from the public gaze.

(18) Groom
(19) Stablehand
(20) Saddlemaker
(21) Arrowmaker
(22) Army cook
(23) Exercise trainer
(24) Army officer
(25) Doctor
(26) Household servant
(27) Bodyguard
(28) Lower-rank samurai

(29) Priest
(30) High-rank samurai
(31) Administrator
(32) Scribe
(33) Visiting shogun.

There were many other servants working in the castle: preparing food, cleaning rooms, washing clothes and keeping the buildings in good repair. Servants were recruited from local peasant families, or from workers living in nearby towns. Their lives were hard and they worked long hours. They had to behave respectfully to the samurai and their families.

The castle was a centre of estate administration, so managers and clerks were busy, inspecting the samurai's farms, collecting taxes and keeping accounts. There were chamberlains to supervise the other servants, scribes to write letters, and messengers to deliver important documents between the samurai and the busy shogun, and, sometimes, the emperor. A castle was also a barracks, where, in peacetime, a garrison of soldiers lived, trained and watched over the neighbouring lands. In war, it became a stronghold; everyone sheltered inside its walls.

CASTLES AND TOWNS

MANY OF JAPAN'S great cities began as castle towns. While daimyo were building their castles, lower-ranking samurai were building houses. It made sense for warriors to stay close to the castle – for safety, and to share in its grandeur. Only samurai homes (and temples) could be built next to castle walls.

New castle towns were carefully planned. Roads, walls, gates, bridges and fresh water supplies were laid out, and areas were 'zoned' for greater and lesser samurai, ordinary soldiers, craftworkers and traders. Many of these people were low-status but they were economically very important because they produced all kinds of everyday goods: pottery, straw sandals, baskets, farm tools, kitchen implements, simple hemp kimonos and fine silk robes. They prepared and sold dried fish, pickled vegetables, rice and millet, tea and wine.

Samurai training encouraged warriors to live pure, self-disciplined lives. But soon, entertainment quarters grew up, where they and all the other town-dwellers could enjoy eating and drinking, relaxing in warm bath-houses, listening to music or going to the theatre.

Japanese people ate mostly rice, vegetables and fish. All round the coasts, fishermen used weighted nets to catch sea-fish, or collected seaweed and shellfish.

21

ENTERTAINING VISITORS

FOR TOP-RANKING samurai, entertaining visitors was an important political duty. A daimyo had great power within his own estates – he could make his own laws, raise his own taxes and even invent his own weights and measures. But, to survive, he needed to make allies from outside, to help him defend his lands when under attack by enemy samurai in times of civil war. Alliances might be made by treaties, through arranged marriages, and by entertaining 'useful' people. Daimyo Hideyoshi (1536–1598) once gave a tea-party for 5,000 guests.

Formal entertainment was a compliment to the nobility and elegance of your guests. You offered them fine food and drink – and carefully arranged the seating plan according to rank, so as not to offend anyone. You might also invite them to share in traditional noble pastimes, such as cherry-blossom viewing or strolling in a beautiful garden to gaze at the full moon, where your guests could express artistic sensitivity by quoting classical poetry.

To entertain a few close friends, you go to a quiet corner of the garden (below) to admire autumn leaves and tell traditional stories, or play the flute. Or you might invite friends to share the Zen Buddhist-inspired tea ceremony.

Through slow, careful ritual, everyone present was encouraged to share moments of tranquil thought. This strengthened the bonds of friendship. But some samurai thought it made people forget their warrior ideals.

Well-educated, wealthy men and women enjoyed writing poetry. Elegant surroundings and fine writing materials added to the pleasure.

Games of skill and strategy, such as backgammon or go, were also popular. Visiting players were welcomed and entertained with great politeness.

Special occasions, such as a visit from a shogun (main picture), involved precise, elaborate ceremony. Knowing the rules of polite society was a sign of samurai rank.

Tea houses (right), built in quiet corners of lovely gardens, were designed to encourage tranquil thoughts among those taking part.

A tray of food is set in front of each guest.

Tea bowl (below) made from pottery known as raku ware. Its simple shape contributed to the tea-ceremony's atmosphere of elegance and calm.

WOMEN'S LIVES

TRADITIONALLY, a woman of the samurai class was brought up to believe that she was inferior to men. It was her duty to serve three masters: her father, her husband and her son. A high-ranking woman had little freedom: marriage was her career; she could not stay single. Her husband was chosen by her parents, as alliances between samurai families were too important to leave to chance.

A wife's first duty was to bear a son to inherit her husband's land. It was also her task to educate her daughters, teaching them suitable manners for polite society, how to read and write, and how to wear elaborate ceremonial clothes.

Samurai women owed their rank – and their safety – to samurai fighting skills.

Some women relied on men to defend them, but others chose to learn martial arts themselves.

Nursemaids cared for young children. They also found time to join in their games, such as flying kites.

Old women and widows led quiet lives. They could offer good advice, but most had little power.

Writing materials:
(A) Brushes
(B) Ink-stone
(C) Block of solid ink
(D) Rice paper.

Women servants worked at many tasks around the castles:
(1) Cleaner
(2) Housemaid
(3) Cook
(4) Ladies' maid.

The work of samurai wives:
(5) Commanding soldiers in their husband's absence
(6) Doing accounts
(7) Giving birth to heirs
(8) Offering prayers as Buddhist nuns.

Some samurai women became poets and novelists; some won praise for their scholarship, or for their holy lives. They fought bravely and intelligently to defend their homes. Hosokawa Jako (1542–1616) climbed up on the roof of her castle to spy on an enemy camp below, then sketched a careful plan of it with her lip-rouge. Women from lower ranks had much more freedom. They became servants, farm labourers and shopkeepers, or helped their husbands with their work.

In towns geisha women worked as companions and skilled entertainers. Samurai men visited them, off-duty, to relax. Many geisha were accomplished musicians, poets and storytellers.

Below:
The Chinese calendar

Boar

Dog

Rat

Ox

Bird

Monkey

Samurai women spent much of their time at home. Unlike ordinary people, they could not wander freely about the streets. Holy days (when they might visit a shrine) or seasonal festivals provided a welcome break from routine.

The main festivals were New Year's Day, Peach Festival, Iris Festival, Weaver Festival and Chrysanthemum Festival. Japanese people measured time using the Chinese calendar, which was based on 12 year-signs, each named after an animal.

Tiger

Hare

Sheep

Horse

Snake

Dragon

Becoming a samurai began at birth. You had to be born to samurai parents or be adopted by them.

As a future member of the army, you could not be left-handed. You were trained to use your right.

You were taught to co-operate unselfishly with other boys. At 7 years old, you went to school.

Aged 10, you spent 12 hours a day at school. You learned to fight, as well as the usual school subjects.

SAMURAI TRAINING

SAMURAI SOLDIERS were young – only 13 or 14. A boy born to a samurai family had been trained for warfare from birth. Like samurai girls, he had no choice; being a warrior was his career.

He was taught two basic skills: how to survive and how to kill. Both involved long, sometimes painful training, using wooden weapons to learn defensive swordplay, and real weapons (thrust into straw mats) when practising the kill. Archery training involved shooting at moving targets, sometimes dogs.

Although your new lifestyle was hard, it included time off to relax.

With other young samurai, you drank warm sake and played go.

The Chinese teacher Lanqi Daolong reached Japan in 1246. He brought with him a new form of Buddhism, called Zen. It soon found favour with the shogun and his samurai.

Experienced warriors and new recruits took part in regular training exercises, to make sure they kept fit and well prepared for battle. One popular form of training was an 'inuomono' (dog-hunt). At other practice sessions, archers mounted on horseback and on foot fired at mock targets fixed in the ground.

You learned about battle techniques and heard stories of past victories from top samurai.

You also learned mental discipline, good manners and respect for older people.

Between 13 and 15, you officially became an adult, after taking part in the genbuku ceremony.

As well as a new, adult, hairstyle (above), you would be given a suit of armour, ready for battle.

You were trained to fight by a senior swordmaster. You had to learn to defend yourself on the battlefield. Your classmates watched your lessons, and it was a disgrace to show any signs of weakness or fear.

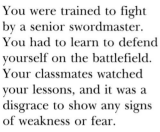

After the 16th century, when guns came to Japan, boys were taught to load, aim and fire – which was far quicker and simpler than training with traditional weapons. To survive, a samurai had to react quickly in battle. High-ranking families prided themselves on their disciplined and intellectual approach to war. Other survival training involved wild horse chases, learning to wrestle wearing armour, and how to fight on horseback. Boys even learned how to tie up prisoners. It was important that they knew the best knots to use so their captives did not escape.

ARMS AND ARMOUR

SAMURAI AND ASHIGARU fought with four main weapons: swords, lances, bows and guns. Bows were long and flexible, made of strips of wood and bamboo bound tightly together. There were at least 12 different types of arrowhead, mostly made of stone. Some were hollow, and whistled as they flew through the air, causing fear and panic. Others were specially sharp to pierce armour, or barbed, to stick in flesh. Lances and bows were carried by ashigaru. The samurai's chosen weapon was a sword. Japanese swordsmiths were so skilful that some swords were credited with superhuman powers. Ancient ritual – as well as technical expertise, rolling and folding fine strips of steel – was involved in their production. Swordsmiths prayed, bathed and purified themselves before making a special blade. Guns were unknown before the 16th century. They were copied, with improvements, from Portuguese arquebuses, brought to Japan by merchants in 1542. They used gunpowder, lit by a smouldering cord, to fire metal shot. Although effective weapons, guns were despised by ancient samurai families.

Hand-to-hand combat was a very important skill. Students were trained by the best swordmasters. Jomyo Meishu was a 12th-century warrior monk. He bravely challenged his enemies and no-one dared to fight him single-handed.

A good suit of armour (below) was one of a samurai's most treasured posessions. He relied on it to help save his life. Samurai armour was skilfully made and beautifully decorated. High-ranking warriors wore suits of plate armour, made of rigid panels of iron laced or riveted together, sometimes combined with chainmail and tough rawhide. Ashigaru wore thinner, lightweight 'folding armour', made of small metal plates.

For a helmet, up to 32 curved metal panels were riveted together and topped with a crest of painted wood. Flexible nape-guards, made of metal strips, protected the neck. Metal face masks – often painted red, for anger – might be added. But they were hot, uncomfortable and made it difficult to see.

Banner with daimyo crest

Samurai swords

Mount for hanging sword from belt

Painted wooden crest

Nape guard

Tachi (long sword worn edge downwards)

Katana (long sword worn edge upwards)

Shoulder armour

Tsuba (guard)

Cuirass (breastplate)

Hand armour

Armoured skirt

A samurai's body was protected by a cuirass – a breastplate with side and back pieces attached (left). His arms and legs were covered by specially shaped panels fitting over shoulders, arms and shins.

Samurai collected as many swords as they could, of different shapes and sizes (above). Prized examples might be looted from enemy dead after a battle.

Below: ashigaru weapons: bow, lances and guns.

Knee protectors

Bow and arrows

Lance

Lance

Lance

Arquebus

Straw sandals

Arquebus

A DAY IN THE LIFE OF A SAMURAI

TAKEDA SHINGEN was a famous samurai. His brother wrote: 'The samurai must never relax his watchfulness. Even when he is alone with his wife, he ought to have his sword by his side.' It was not that samurai women were untrustworthy, but that a samurai must always put his warrior duty first, even before the people he loves.

In peacetime, life for many lower-ranking samurai was pleasantly routine: guard duty, battle training and regular patrols, plus the daily comforts of home life.

7 am (dawn) Rises and dresses, ties hair in topknot. Rolls bedding mat away.

7.30 am Breakfasts with his wife and children: rice and pickled vegetables.

8 am Makes his way through the town streets to the castle.

9 am Lookout duty. With other low-rank samurai, he patrols the top of the castle walls.

1 pm After lunch, it is time for fitness training. Practises swordfighting with expert teacher.

3 pm Leaves castle to visit local craftsman who is mending some of his armour.

30

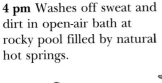

4 pm Washes off sweat and dirt in open-air bath at rocky pool filled by natural hot springs.

5 pm Clean and purified, he can visit the Buddhist temple nearby to pray.

8 pm Dinner break in the castle hall along with other samurai: they eat fish, soup and rice.

11 pm Time to go home. His wife greets him and tells him what she and the children have done all day.

12 midnight Bedtime. But before sleep, time to sit quietly and meditate. How well has he performed his tasks as a samurai today?

10 pm Guard-duty over, relaxing with samurai friends.

In wartime, everything changed. A samurai had to follow his daimyo lord' into battle. He would spend weeks, perhaps months, living rough in wild country and facing enemy ambushes, disease and exhaustion. The chances were that, sooner or later, he would be killed. We do not know exactly how many samurai survived to a ripe old age, but the casualty figures for most samurai battles were horrendous.

NEW SAMURAI STYLE

TRADITIONALLY, SAMURAI had little interest in the arts, religion and philosophy. Craft skills, except swordmaking and calligraphy, were considered lower-class. A warrior should buy the best armour, and proudly wear a surcoat with his family crest, but brightly coloured clothes and furnishings were for actors and women.

But in 1576, samurai Oda Nobunaga seized control of Japan, burning down ancient Buddhist temples because priests were a threat to his rule. Then he began to build a castle at Azuchi.

Decorative techniques: To make a fine spray of paint, balance a wet paintbrush across your wrist and flick sharply.

To apply gold leaf:
(1) Beat gold wire until it flattens and spreads into little flakes.

(2) Rub dry paintbrush in hair so it will become charged with static electricity.

(3) Hold the paintbrush over the gold flakes. The static will make them 'jump' onto the brush.

(4) Hold brush over the painting. Tap handle; the gold flakes will drop and attach to the painting.

Above:
Patterned silk kimono, 17th century.

Sliding doors (right) with a coloured ink drawing of a crane (a bird, symbol of long life) and pine trees. Painted by Kano Eitoku, in 1566.

To decorate the castle, Nobunaga employed Japan's best painters. Long years of civil war were coming to an end, and samurai began to have time and money to spend on things other than war. As we have seen, they soon copied Nobunaga's ideas, and a new samurai style – bold, bright and using luxurious materials – became popular. It was copied for male and female clothing, especially for loose robes called kosode or kimono, and for weapons and armour, too. Formal clothes, for the shogun's or emperor's court, were still traditionally simple and dark-coloured.

Above:
A decorated lacquer box.

Left:
A samurai saddle made of leather and wood.

Elaborate armour (right), made in 1859, at the end of the samurai period. It is constructed of gold-lacquered iron and held together with silk thread. The sleeves and legs are chain-mail, and the boots are made of fur. The helmet has an iron mask, decorated with animal hair.

Metal crest

Iron helmet

Iron face mask

Neck guard

Shoulder guard made of metal plates

Animal-hair whiskers

Throat protector

Leather breastplate

Silk cord

Metal plates

Metal shin protectors

Fur boots

AT THE THEATRE

WHEN SHOGUN TOKUGAWA IEYASU invited a group of high-ranking samurai to dinner in his castle in 1603, he arranged for a Noh play to be performed to entertain them. Like many samurai, he had a specially built Noh stage.

Noh plays were ancient and traditional. The book telling Noh actors how to perform was written in 1400; its instructions were followed for centuries.

Masks worn by Noh actors:
(1) Calm young woman
(2) Joyful old man
(3) Kindly old man
(4) Woman betrayed by her lover
(5) Deserted woman driven mad by jealousy
(6) Angry warrior.

Noh actors changed and made up in the dressing room, then sat in the 'mirror room' to meditate and prepare for the coming performance.

Dressing room and mirror room

Painted screen

Covered passageway

Main stage

A   B   C   D   E   F   G

The first Noh plays were performed at shrines, often in front of sacred trees. The screen behind each Noh stage was painted with an old pine tree, as a reminder of Noh drama's religious origins.

Traditionally, Noh theatres had a square stage with space for the orchestra behind. The audience sat in an open-air stand.

Kabuki actors had to be versatile. The Japanese artist Utagawa Toyokuni, who lived in the 18th century, drew this series of costumes to show all the different kinds of parts an actor might have to play during his career:
(A) Daiymo
(B) Shogun
(C) Town-dweller
(D) Low-rank samurai
(E) Army commander
(F) Master swordsman
(G) Woman.

Noh actors – all men – did not try to appear true to life. In some ways, they resembled samurai themselves: powerful, well-trained, disciplined and formal. Actors wore masks and heavy costumes; the spirit of each mask was meant to inspire them. On stage, they used stiff, stylised gestures to tell the audience what was happening. For example, gently moving a sleeve meant 'I am falling in love.' Music and dance sustained the dramatic mood.

Another type of drama, Kabuki, was performed in castle towns from the 17th century. It was a complete contrast to Noh plays: action-packed, loud with songs and speeches, full of dramatic fights, brave heroines and dastardly villains. Some shoguns tried to ban Kabuki, but it was too popular.

By the 18th century, wealthy spectators at Kabuki plays were sheltered by tiled roofs. Some also paid for private boxes, screened by bamboo blinds, where they could meet friends – or even lovers. The shoguns did not approve.

Side stage for chorus

A WARLORD AND HIS ARMY

LIKE THE REST OF JAPANESE SOCIETY, samurai armies were strictly ordered by rank. Commanders came from the samurai class. They were expected to arrive for battle with a pre-arranged number of fully equipped fighting men. The size of each private army depended on how much land a samurai had. His wealth was measured in koku – the amount of rice needed to feed one man for a year. A commander was expected to provide six soldiers per 100 koku. We can judge the vastness of some samurai estates by the size of their armies: for example, in 1587, the Shimazu family attacked Minamata castle with around 100,000 soldiers – equivalent to over a million koku of land.

On the march, armies slept where they could (officers in temples or farmhouses, ordinary soldiers in barns or under bushes). When the battle site was reached, they pitched tents inside a circle of tobari (camp-curtains) – proud banners displaying the daimyo's crest.

Samurai fighting skills:
(A) Archer
(B) Arquebusier (gunner)
(C) Spearman
(D) Flag-bearer
(E) Army commander
(F) Bodyguard
(G) Footsoldier.

Dressing for battle:
(1) Put on loincloth.
(2) Add short kimono.
(3) Tie baggy trousers around waist.
(4) Fasten shin pads.
(5) Fix thigh guards.
(6) Add chain-mail sleeves.
(7) Add chest guard.
(8) Buckle on body armour (breastplate, backplate and skirt). Then fasten with silk cord.
(9) Cover hair with scarf.
(10) Tie on helmet. Arrange shoulder guards and face mask.

A B C D E F G

Armies were divided into separate camps, each led by a senior samurai and staffed by officers, banner-carriers, cooks, baggage-handlers, straw-sandal-carriers and grooms (for the warhorses). Commanders had their own personal staff including guards for the treasure chest, hat-carriers and pages. There were signallers (who sent messages with drums and gongs) and doctors. These only treated senior men, so ordinary soldiers relied on folk-remedies such as eating horse-dung to stop bleeding, or bathing their wounds in their own heated urine to ease pain.

Victorious troops rode back to camp carrying the heads of enemies they had killed in battle. It was more honourable for defeated soldiers to be killed – even like this – than to survive.

ON PATROL

EVEN IN PEACETIME, a samurai soldier spent some of his time out on patrol, defending estate boundaries. In wartime, armies advanced on foot, surviving as best they could in hostile lands. In dangerous situations, they might rely on knowledge learned from books on warfare. *The Art of War*, a book written by Chinese general Sun Tzu between 450 and 421 BC, advised: 'Birds rising in flight ahead are a sign that the enemy is waiting to ambush you.'

Life on patrol might be exciting, but it was hard and tiring, too. Soldiers had to carry everything they needed, and wore their heavy armour all the time. It soon became smelly and infested with fleas and lice which had to be 'smoked' out over a hot fire. Essential supplies included spare weapons, matches and gunpowder, strong thread for repairing armour, fresh straw sandals and a change of underwear, plus a straw mat for a bed. Food was mostly 'instant' rice, cooked and dried before setting out. On patrol it would be reconstituted by adding hot water – boiled in a metal helmet. It might be flavoured with dried tuna, which was light and easy to carry, but soldiers also tried to catch 'stamina foods': rabbit and wild deer.

In wartime, everything needed by a samurai army had to be light and easy to carry. As well as food, weapons and armour, soldiers also carried a portable Buddhist shrine, which could be set up in the army camp and used to provide a place of worship and meditation. Samurai believed this helped them to fight better.

Long, narrow flags, called nobori, were carried into battle. Each flag was decorated with a daimyo's crest. If soldiers became scattered on the battlefield, the flags helped them to locate their comrades again.

Originally, the flags were fastened just to the top of a T-shaped wooden pole. By around 1500, each flag was laced down one side as well. This stopped them flapping and made the crests easier to read at a distance.

Flags were often carried by ashigaru (ordinary soldiers). Each samurai army had dozens of flag-bearers. Carrying a flag could be dangerous as bearers had to stay close to the army commanders,

sometimes right in the heart of the battle. The flag was fixed to each bearer's back. This left both his hands free for fighting, but also made him a conspicuous target for enemy arrows.

CASTLE UNDER SIEGE

THE ARCHITECTS who designed samurai castles used nawabari (stretched cords) to lay out the earthworks, moats and stone walls that defended every castle keep. These barriers were essential to protect against enemy attack, three being the ideal, but each castle varied, according to its site. Barriers stopped besieging armies getting close enough to attack defenders sheltering inside the wood and plaster keep. A skilled bowman could shoot an arrow 380 metres (415 yards); an arquebus could kill at almost 500 metres (550 yards).

Watchtower

Water-filled moats were a useful way of defending a castle. They stopped outer walls being undermined and made it easy to shoot at enemies trying to sail across in boats. But water could be used to attack castles too. In 1538, the samurai Toyotomi Hideyoshi ordered his troops to build a dam across a river close to Kameyama castle, which he was besieging. As the flood waters rose, the castle's defenders surrendered.

Besieging troops

Castle moat

If an army breached the outer defences, the keep was almost certain to be destroyed. Fire was the great hazard – the keep's wooden frame was highly inflammable. But even if the outer defences held, a besieged castle's inhabitants might face slow death from starvation or disease unless allies arrived to attack the besiegers from the rear. On the greatest samurai estates, minor castles were built all around the boundaries as a first line of defence and as barracks for 'rescue' troops.

Besiegers crossing a moat risked being hit by gunfire or arrows before reaching the castle. So half the soldiers sheltered at the back of the boat, ready to renew the attack if the men at the front were shot down.

Castle yard

Slit window
protects archer but
allows arrows to
be fired

THE SAMURAI ERA ENDS

AFTER 1603, the Tokugawa shoguns ruling Japan gradually tamed all the warlike samurai families. After 1649, daimyo status depended not on fame and good fortune in war, but on the number of soldiers a samurai could provide for national defence. It was as if samurai had become state servants, no longer the proud, independent warriors of old.

The Tokugawa shogun's new policies of peace at home and isolation from abroad negated the need for samurai fighting skills. Samurai kept their rank, their traditions and their estates, but were increasingly futile. Their wealth dwindled, as towns flourished, and low-ranking merchants, craftworkers and entertainers grew rich.

The 1868 revolution deposed the Tokugawa shoguns and the imperial system was restored after a lapse of more than 250 years. Emperor Meiji rapidly introduced a policy of westernisation, making samurai traditions seem even more archaic. But to many Japanese the old samurai ideals of honour, bravery, loyalty and self-sacrifice remained a noble inspiration.

Pair of screens showing Japan (above) and the rest of the world (below) by a Japanese artist of the Edo period (1603–1868).

Samurai Rokuemon Tsunenaga (right) led a Japanese trading voyage to America and Europe in 1613, but the project failed.

During the 17th and 18th centuries, when Japan was closed to foreigners, Japanese ships like this (right) sailed from Nagasaki to trade with the outside world.

Nagasaki, with its splendid natural harbour, was Japan's main port. This is how it was pictured on a late 17th-century map.

Rokuemon Tsunenaga

Commodore Matthew Perry, commander of the fleet of American 'black ships' (warships) that reached Japan in 1853.

Right:
Rich costume and warlike make-up defined a samurai in the Kabuki plays. But by the 19th century, few samurai were wealthy or skilled warriors.

The western-style Mitsui building in Tokyo (above) was built in 1872 for a company founded by a samurai-turned-merchant.

As well as providing good physical training, Japanese martial arts (below) also aim to encourage self-discipline and high moral standards.

Above: Continuing tradition. Picture of a pilot with a samurai sword from a Japanese wartime magazine, 1939–1945.

Japanese martial arts, like Kendo (The Way of the Sword, right), Judo (The Way of Gentleness) and Karate (The Empty Hand Way) have become popular sports in many countries.

SOME FAMOUS SAMURAI

Prince Yamato, the first samurai

Prince Yamato is said to have lived about 100 BC, and to have been the son of Emperor Keiko. Many stories were told of his brave adventures. He was fearless (he fought and defeated many of the emperor's enemies), ruthless (he killed his brother for turning up late to a meal) and cunning (he disguised himself as an old woman to get inside a rebel's castle). He received help from the gods – his aunt was high priestess of the sun goddess. He owned a magic sword, made from a serpent's tail. He was the best fighter of his age.

But sadly, Yamato may only be a legendary figure: a combination of several real warriors' adventures, mixed with ancient religious beliefs.

The Soga Revolution

The Soga family were rich, noble warriors with friends – and enemies – at the emperor's court. They wanted to 'modernise' the way Japan was governed by introducing new ideas borrowed from China. But other noble families disagreed. So, in AD 587, Soga warriors fought a battle at Shigisen, and won. In 592, one of the family, Prince Shotoku, became emperor. He passed many new laws, transforming the way the country was run.

Fujiwara: samurai wives and mothers

Soga rule did not last long. In 645 another warrior family – the Fujiwara – became even more powerful at court. They did not become emperors, but for the next 1,200 years, Fujiwara women played a very important role. They married emperors and gave birth to heirs to the throne. Between 724 and 1900, 54 of the 76 Japanese emperors had Fujiwara mothers.

Otomo Yakamochi, the first shogun

Otomo Yakamochi lived in the 8th century. Although not a very effective warrior – the Emperor Kammu called him an 'incompetent coward' – he was the first warrior to receive the title of shogun.

Minamoto Tametomo, the great archer

Minamoto Tametomo lived in the 12th century. At 17, he had become famous for his skill with his bow and arrows. A contemporary chronicle reported that he fought over 20 battles in under two years, and captured dozens of castles. Tametomo's bow-arm was said to be 10 centimetres (4 inches) longer than his other arm. In 1170 he became the first samurai to commit ritual sacrifice (seppuku) rather than face defeat. Many samurai followed his example.

Tomoe Gozen

Lady Tomoe Gozen was the wife of a powerful samurai, Minamoto Yoshinaka. In 1180 she fought alongside her husband in the battle of Uji. Bravely, she tried to fight off the enemy soldiers while he attempted to commit suicide. Gozen survived the battle, but retired to a Buddhist monastery and became a nun.

The end of the Taira

The Taira family were the most powerful samurai in 12th-century Japan; they ruled on behalf of the 8-year-old emperor Antoku. But they were defeated at the sea-battle of Dan-no-ura in 1185. They had no choice but mass suicide. Led by Antoku's grandmother, carrying him in her arms, all the leading Taira warriors jumped overboard in their armour, and drowned.

Minamoto Yoritomo, first shogun for life

Minamoto Yoritomo won the Gempei War. After many struggles against the other samurai family who had helped defeat the Taira, he now controlled the country and the emperor. In 1192, the old emperor died and Go-Toba came to the throne. He was only 13. He knew he had to remain friends with Yoritomo to keep the throne, and ensure peace for his country. So he made him shogun for life, with the right to pass on the title, and its powers, to his sons.

Kusunoki Masahige, the loyal samurai

Most samurai were loyal only to their own families. Kusunoki Masahige became famous for his support of Emporer Go-Diago, who came to power in 1318. Go-Diago was one of the few Japanese emperors who wanted to stand up to the shoguns and rule for himself. Kusunoki Masahige gave him wise advice, but he was overruled by courtiers, who had none of his samurai skills. However, he chose loyally to obey the emperor's orders, and was killed in battle.

Oda Nobunaga, warlord and diplomat

Nobunaga (1534–1582) came from a low-ranking samurai family, but was so skilful as an army commander that he soon became rich and famous. He fought many battles, but he also sought power through diplomacy and marriage alliances. He encouraged Christian missionaries to undermine the power of warlike Buddhist monks. He built the huge clifftop Azuchi castle, on the shores of a lake, as the base from which he could rule all Japan. But soon afterwards, he died in a temple fire that was started deliberately.

Toyotomi Hideyoshi: the last great samurai?

Toyotomi Hideyoshi continued Nobunaga's quest to unite the warring samurai under a single strong ruler. Through great skill and bravery in battle, he succeeded in defeating his last rivals in 1590. He also tried to take all weapons away from peasants and farmers, in case they rebelled. He built a magnificent castle at Osaka, and led a disastrous invasion of Korea. He was never made shogun as his family were too low-ranking. But until his death in 1598, he was the most powerful man in Japan. After his death, Hideyoshi was betrayed by his friend the samurai Tokugawa Ieyasu, who had promised to act as guardian for his young son. Instead, in 1603, Ieyasu seized power for himself, and founded a dynasty of shoguns that ruled for over 250 years.

GLOSSARY

Arquebus An early form of shotgun. It used gunpowder to fire small metal shot.

Ashigaru An ordinary soldier in a samurai army, not of samurai rank.

Barbed Armed with spikes.

Bath-house A place where men went to relax by bathing, often communally, in tubs of water, sometimes heated by natural springs. Food, drink and music were also available.

Buddhist A follower of the religious teachings of the Indian philosopher-king Gautama Siddhartha (6th century BC), later known as Buddha. Buddhists aim to live pure, honest, simple lives, trying to follow the 'right path' that would lead them to God. Many Japanese people were Buddhists; others followed the ancient Shinto religion.

Bugyo An overseer or commissioner, in charge of castle building operations.

Burdock A plant with large round leaves.

Burdock piling A way of building walls with large boulders.

Calligraphy Beautiful handwriting, a prized samurai art.

Chamberlain A senior servant, in charge of running a castle household.

Classical Traditional and respected.

Daimyo Lord: a title given to top-ranking, wealthy, powerful samurai who owned castles and great estates.

Disordered piling A way of building walls using small, rough stones packed together.

Gables Pointed roof-ends. Elaborate roofs on Japanese castles were a sign of rank and high status.

Geisha Professional women entertainers who provided companionship for men.

Go An ancient game for two players, rather like the modern game 'Othello'. Black and white stones are placed on a board with the aim of surrounding the largest area.

Hemp A plant with tough fibres that can be woven into coarse cloth.

Husk The outer, papery covering of rice and other grains.

Intellectual Concerned with thoughts and ideas.

Inuomono A dog-hunt, an army training exercise using dogs as moving targets.

Judo A Japanese martial art (the 'Way of Gentleness').

Kabuki Lively, popular Japanese drama.

Karate A Japanese martial art (the 'Empty Hand Way' – no weapons are used).

Kendo A Japanese martial art (the 'Way of the Sword').

Kimono A Japanese garment with wrap-over front and wide sleeves.

Koku A measure of wealth: the amount of rice needed to feed one man for a year.

Lacquer A precious substance used to decorate fine objects or buildings. It comes from the sap of a Far Eastern tree.

Lance A long-handled spear.

Nawabari 'Stretched cord', the method, using ropes and pegs, of marking a castle's layout on the ground.

Nobori A flag or banner carried by a soldier.

Noh An ancient, upper-class drama.

Pavilions Small, elegant buildings, usually in gardens.

Prefabricated Ready-made, in sections that can be assembled later.

Ritual Precise, elaborate ceremony, often with a religious or political meaning.

Samurai A warrior, member of the Japanese upper class. Most powerful from the 12th to the 17th centuries.

Shinto The ancient, traditional religion of Japan, based on reverence for nature-spirits.

Shogun The title of the military ruler of Japan between the 12th and 19th centuries.

Surcoat A loose robe, worn over armour.

Tatami Floor mats, used for sitting and sleeping.

Tenshu The strong central tower (keep) of a castle.

Tobari 'Camp-curtains', banners surrounding an army camp.

Zen A branch of the Buddhist religion popular in Japan, especially among samurai. It stresses mental discipline and self-control.

Zoned Divided into regions (zones), each with a different purpose.

INDEX

Page numbers in bold refer to illustrations.

First published in MCMXCV as *Inside Story: A Samurai Castle* by Macdonald Young Books © The Salariya Book Co Ltd MCMXCV